I0078584

Frontline Worshipper

Devotional

Julia A. Royston

Edited by:
Claude R. Royston

BK Royston Publishing
Jeffersonville, IN

BK Royston Publishing

P. O. Box 4321

Jeffersonville, IN 47131

www.juliaroyston.com

Phone: 502-802-5385

© 2011 Julia A. Royston

All rights reserved.

No part of this book may be reproduced, stored in a retrieval system, or transmitted by means without the written permission of the author.

First published by BK Royston Publishing

Cover Design by: Julia A. Royston

Logo Designed by: Jonathan Snorten

ISBN-13: 978-0-9818135-8-5

ISBN-10: 0-9818135-8-5

Printed in the United States of America

Other Titles by Julia A. Royston

A New Season in Word: Inspirations for Divine Living

© 2007

How Hot is Your Love Life? Return to Your First Love

© 2008

Everyday Miracles-© 2010

Frontline Worshipper—© 2011

Music by Julia A. Royston

Joy in His Presence – © 2004

Hymns for Him – © 2005

A New Season in Word and Song – © 2007

For Your Glory Lord—© 2009

Everyday Miracles—©2010

Published by juju 4ee Publishing

Acknowledgements

I thank my Lord and Savior Jesus Christ for giving me another opportunity to introduce more people to you. I thank you that you have entrusted this gift to me. Lord, let your Spirit move through this book to the people who will read it. Empower your people with the power to continue to fight on the frontline.

To my husband, Brian K. Royston, the love of my life for loving me so much and cheering me on so that I can be and do all that God has placed in me. I love you...

Thanks to all of my family for their love and support.

A special thank you to Rev. Claude R. Royston for using his fine tooth comb to edit this book.

I dedicate this book to every "Frontline Worshipper" who ministers in the prison house, store front, stadium, cathedral or hut. God Bless You in all that you for the King and His Kingdom.

Introduction

On the battlefield, we can get tired, weary and discouraged. This devotional book is designed to encourage, uplift and provide daily spiritual sustenance that you need to fight on. Being a worship leader, dancer, actor, actress, director, vocalist, poet or spoken word artists is difficult at times. There is a demand on your gift and spirit. But, know that God is with you to give you the power to use you for His glory. Don't give up. Don't be dismayed. God will bless you for your service until. "Therefore, I urge you, brothers and sisters, in view of God's mercy, to offer your bodies as a living sacrifice, holy and pleasing to God—this is your true and proper worship." Romans 12:1 (NIV)

Keep fighting on the frontline for the victory is already yours. God Bless You!

Julia Royston

Table of Contents

FRONTLINE
WORSHIPPER

"When Jesus saw him lie, and knew that he had been now a long time in that case, he saith unto him, Wilt thou be made whole?" John 5:6 (KJV)

"Now it's time to change your ways! Turn to face God so he can wipe away your sins, pour out showers of blessing to refresh you…" Acts 3:19 (The Message translation)

A Challenge to Change

Every day our lives are impacted by the changes in legislation, employment and society. In most cases, we have no control over these changes. If we keep a job, we go along with the change at work. Our government does not always ask us how we feel about the laws but, we have to abide by them. No matter how we dread it, change is constant and inevitable. I participated in an event with the theme, "Challenge 2 Change". This was an outreach to the community with a message of a better life through Christ but, with the question, "are you up to the challenge?" Are you willing to take the "Challenge 2 Change"? Even if you are a Christian, is God challenging you to say yes to make changes in your life?

God is a gentleman and it is our choice. Daily we must accept the challenge, ask God for guidance, His Spirit and direction to be like Him. Fortunately, God's changes are for our betterment. Even though we may not like the changes, in the end, we will be better people, Christians and live the abundant life He died for us to live. Are you up for the challenge? Jesus asked people over and over in scripture; do you want to be made whole? This was a challenge to those who were sick to accept the change to wholeness. The changes that you make for God will bring wholeness and healing to your life. Are you up for the challenge? Will you make the change?

Challenge: Make a list of changes that you know need to be made in your life. Pray for strength to make these changes. Write out a plan for making these changes. If necessary, seek professionals to help you make these changes and then do it. Your best life is still ahead.

Thought for the Day:

God will give you power to overcome any challenge if you ask Him for strength, power and boldness.

<u>Reflection</u>

"For it is God which worketh in you both to will and to do of his good pleasure." Philippians 2:13

A Want To Attitude

I cannot tell you how many times a day that I hear the words, "I don't want to" from students that I teach. What do you say to that? As the teacher, I must take the extra effort to find something to motivate them. So I offer incentives and options as encouragement for them to do the work. If however, it is a fun activity, games or play time, there is no hesitation for the "want to" from each student. Each student becomes excited and loud. They cheer, clap their hands or leap for joy at the thought of doing something that they "want to do." There was an older member of our church that used to say "you gotta' have a "want to" down in you to live this Christian life." Do you have a "want to" down in you to live a life pleasing to God? Do you have a "want to" in you to go to work each day? Some of you may say "yes" to really having a desire to "want to".

But, a REAL "want to" makes you do something different. A REAL "want to" makes you evaluate every procedure, policy, project and person in your life. A REAL "want to" makes sure that all systems are operating smoothly to be able to live the abundant life. Now think about it. Do you really "want to?" If you do, God's favor will be poured out over your holy "want to."

Thought for the Day:

Watch the miraculous manifest in your life when you say "yes" and do what God wants you to do.

FRONTLINE
WORSHIPPER

Reflection

_____

_____

_____

_____

_____

_____

_____

_____

_____

_____

_____

_____

_____

_____

_____

_____

_____

_____

_____

_____

_____

"He took the blind man by the hand and led him outside the village. When he had spit on the man's eyes
and put his hands on him, Jesus asked, "Do you see anything?" He looked up and said, "I see people; they
look like trees walking around." 25Once more Jesus
put his hands on the man's eyes. Then his eyes were
opened, his sight was restored, and he saw everything
clearly." Mark 8:23-25 (KJV)

Adjust Your Focus

I recently went to the eye doctor for an exami-
nation. I told the doctor that I now hold a piece
of paper further away from my eyes in order to
get good focus. He said, at my age, my range of
focus has changed. Are you having trouble focusing on the things that are most important in
your life? Do you resist focusing clearly on situations because they are difficult or painful?
Do you become overwhelmed while looking at
the entire situation? Well, adjust your focus:

1. Focus on what is going right. Celebrate these accomplishments and share them.

2. Focus on the problem that you can change
   or

have some control over.

3. Focus on the smaller, manageable pieces first and then on the larger more difficult tasks later. The larger more difficult tasks may require additional assistance so ask for help.

4. Do not focus on the things that are unrelated to your situation and out of your control. Placing your focus on those things is a waste of time, energy and resources.

5. Focus on yourself and not your neighbor. People spend so much time on what their neighbor is doing and they never get around to focusing on themselves and how they can be their best.

6. Remove any distractions that prohibit or limit your ability to focus and this includes people.

Know that the object of your focus, concentration and attention will change periodically. Be ready to make the switch quickly without hesitation. Concentration on the wrong thing is as detrimental as no concentration at all.

Thought of the Day:

Focus your physical and spiritual eyes on God and watch Him do thing beyond your wildest dreams.

<u>Reflection</u>

_____

_____

_____

_____

_____

_____

_____

_____

_____

_____

_____

_____

_____

_____

_____

_____

_____

_____

_____

_____

"And, behold, God himself is with us for our captain, and his priests with sounding trumpets to cry alarm against you. O children of Israel, fight ye not against the LORD God of your fathers; for ye shall not prosper. 13But Jeroboam caused an ambushment to come about behind them: so they were before Judah, and the ambushment was behind them." 2 Chronicles 13:12-14, 16 (KJV)

Ambushed but, Victorious

The children of Israel found themselves in a battle completely surrounded by the enemy. They were prepared to face the enemy in front but, the enemy also came from behind. In the scriptures, this is called an ambushment. (KJV) Have you ever been in a situation that felt like it was an ambush? You have trouble coming from all sides, i.e. the front, the sides and the worst, from behind. The trouble that comes from behind is the unexpected and it blindsides you like a sucker punch. You know a sucker punch is one that is below the belt or from the back of the head where you are vulnerable and least protected.

The enemy wants to catch you off guard and destroy you in an unfair fight. But, greater is he that is within you than he that is in the world. In this instance, the enemy had been warned not to come against the armies of God but, Jeroboam knew they were small and out-numbered. But, Jeroboam underestimated their God. In this passage, we find four things to consider about being ambushed.

God is with us. – If God is for us, who can be against us? Jeroboam was warned not to fight the children of Israel because their God was with them. No matter what you face always re-member that God is with you. No matter how outnumbered you are in the ambush, God is on your side.

God is our captain – In verse 12 of 2 Chroni-cles, the children of Israel reminded the enemy that God is our captain. With God as the cap-tain, you have the best strategist and one with all power. He knows the enemy best and can defeat him.

God will not lose and your enemy will not win. God will win every time. It may seem that your enemy is winning but, know that God has the final say and will win every time.

God delivered them and they were victorious. In the midst of the ambush, God delivered His people from the enemy. If you trust in God and follow His instructions, you will be victorious every time.

Thought of the Day:

God is the God of victory. The greater the attack the greater will be the victory.

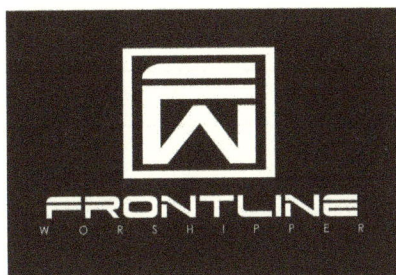

Reflection

"And Joshua said unto the people, Sanctify yourselves: for tomorrow the LORD will do wonders among you." Joshua 3:5 (KJV)

Are You Ready?

Bishop T. D. Jakes introduced his ministry to the nations by stating, "Get Ready, Get Ready, Get Ready!" Over the years we have associated this phrase with Bishop Jakes. But I ask you, are you really ready for what God is about to do in your life? Often my husband asks me the same question. Of course I say I'm ready. But, in my quiet time, I have to ask God to prepare me and make me ready for what He has in my life. The scripture says "He is able to do exceedingly and abundantly above all we can ask or think." (Ephesians 3:20 KJV) The amazing thing is that God is about to do some things for His people that we haven't even thought about or asked for yet. That in itself is mind boggling. Joshua and the children of Israel found themselves standing on the brink of a promise from God.

God told Joshua to tell the people to "sanctify yourselves" because tomorrow God was about to do some wondrous things in their midst. The word sanctify in this instance meant get your house and yourself in order for what God was about to do. God had made a promise and He was about to make good on His promise. You must realize that if God makes a promise He will do it, ready or not. Are you ready? Are you ready physically, mentally and emotionally to accept what God has in store for you? Be prepared to cast aside old mind sets and old habits as you enter into new places and positions based upon the promises of God. Think about what God promised and now look at your current situation, are you ready?

Thought of Day:

God always keeps His promises. Your job is to get yourself ready for what He is about to do.

Reflection

_____

_____

_____

_____

_____

_____

_____

_____

_____

_____

_____

_____

_____

_____

_____

_____

_____

_____

_____

_____

_____

"The Israelites went up to Bethel and inquired of God."
Judges 20:18 (NIV)

"Let us therefore come boldly unto the throne of
grace..." Hebrews 4:15 (KJV)

Ask the Boss

If there is a task or problem that arises at work,
I make every effort to ask my boss, "how do
you want the assignment done or situation
handled?" I don't feel like I am an incompetent
person or that my opinions or expertise are not
important but, I am not the boss. It saves me
time and effort doing it the way the boss wants
it done rather than going my own way. Additionally, it saves me the embarrassment of
apologizing for making a mistake later. Many
years ago, the Lord spoke to me and said, "You
work for me." I realized then that God was my
boss. He wanted to be consulted, advised and
considered when I made any decisions. Looking back, I realize that He was about to assign
new tasks in new places with new people.

This was the ultimate obedience test. Would I obey God completely? Yes, I did but, will you? Will you allow God to be head and the boss of your life? In normal situations, when you consistently obey the boss, complete tasks in a timely and excellent manner and do not create chaos in a work environment, you receive a promotion or are trusted with new assignments. God is the supreme boss and can take your life well beyond any supervisor, boss or executive, if you obey Him. God has a great plan for your life and can make the plan a reality. So watch God do the incredible in your life if you will just go in prayer and ask the boss.

Thought of Day:

The throne of God is always open to you. God's ear is always listening for your slightest cry. Don't hesitate to ask Him anything, anytime day or night.

Reflection

_____

_____

_____

_____

_____

_____

_____

_____

_____

_____

_____

_____

_____

_____

_____

_____

_____

_____

_____

_____

"To this end was I born, and for this cause came I into the world..." John 18:37

Born for This

Jesus' actual ministry on earth was only 3 years in duration. He packed a lot of teaching, healing and deliverance in those three years. Those three years turned the world and the lives of many upside down. But, when Jesus stood before Pilate to be accused, tortured and sentenced to crucifixion, he proclaimed that this was the reason he came into the world. All of the miracles, teaching and impartation done by Jesus were an essential part of His ministry. Although the crucifixion, was what He was born and came to this earth to do. Jesus was born to die. What an oxymoron? Prior to this text, Jesus was agonizing over the cross in the garden. It was a tough decision but, this was His "born for this" event and moment. This is called living or fulfilling your purpose, i.e. "the purpose driven life." If you haven't experienced this, keep living.

Music and singing is what I enjoy the most and it is a natural gift that I pray will bless many. I thought music was my "born for this" assignment. But I was notified the other day by God that I was born to teach. I must confess that I wish He had told me that I was born to sing because singing is much easier for me. I am a teacher by profession but, teaching requires energy, concentration, creativity and the preparation that can be tedious. I have to pray for guidance, ideas and revise and rethink everything I do before each lesson. When singing, I stand and deliver with ease. For me it is like breathing. It is not that I don't need God to sing, I just need Him so much more when I teach. Everyone is given an innate gift or talent whether it is cooking, music or working with your hands, we all have at least one.

The difference between a "born for this" assignment and a natural gift or talent is that the "born for this assignment" will take God alone to help you to accomplish or perform it.

The "born for this" tasks are only fulfilled with God, through God, for God and God should be the only one who gets the credit. Some time, the "born for this assignment" is your least desired but, most rewarding because you are in God's perfect and divine will. What is your "born for this" assignment?

Thought for the Day:

Be willing to die doing what you born for.

Reflection

_____

_____

_____

_____

_____

_____

_____

_____

_____

_____

_____

_____

_____

_____

_____

_____

_____

_____

"I have put my words in your mouth and covered you with the shadow of my hand.." Isaiah 51:16 (NIV)

"Keep me as the apple of your eye; hide me in the shadow of your wings." Psalm 17:8 (NIV)

Covered

I cannot sleep unless I have a comforter, sheet or blanket. I must have some type of covering over me when I sleep. In the midst of sleeping, if the covers slip off, I will awaken and cover up the area that has become uncovered. I especially don't like my feet out from under the covers. There is a popular expression, "I got you covered." This means that you are willing to help out a friend if they are short of cash or if they get in a fight, you "got their back." "I got you covered" in church means that you are covering this person with prayer. Did you know that God is covering you as well? In Isaiah 51:16, God said I have covered you with the shadow of my hand. David said in Psalm 17, "hide me in the shadow of your wings." God has us covered.

We are under God's protection, His watchful eye and in His loving care. It is interesting that we are under the shadow of His hand or wings. If we were completely covered, we would suffocate and die. God wants us to know that He is there surrounding us. The only way we can get from under His covering is if we leave. Don't leave your feet, head or hands from God's protection. Know that you are covered to be blessed. You are covered to be used for His Glory. If you ever feel alone, rest in the knowledge that God has you covered.

Thought of the Day:

God's protection is as comforting as a blanket on a winter night.

FRONTLINE
WORSHIPPER

Reflection

"Forget the former things; do not dwell on the past. See, I am doing a new thing!" Isaiah 43:18-19 (NIV)

Discontinue and Pursue God's New

Some department stores have bi-annual sales on specific items in their inventory. I enjoy waiting for these sales because I purchase the items I need at a reduced price. For the bargain price, I will wait six months. In December, the bi-annual sale was advertised and I went to the store. Upon entering, I noticed that the items that I wanted to buy and had waited until now to buy were not in the store. I asked the sales clerk for assistance and she replied, "we have discontinued that item and no longer carry it in our inventory." I was told apologetically, that the item I wanted wasn't profitable for the company and they "discontinued" it. I was horrified that no one from the front office bothered to tell me that they were discontinuing my favorite item.

I had saved my money for that purchase. Okay, I am kidding but, I was disappointed and upset. I realized that I would have to start all over again to find a "New" style of the item, that I liked, it fit and I could afford. At times, we all need to take an inventory of our lives and see what needs to be discontinued. Someone else is not going to make that decision to discontinue some things in your life, it is up to you. If you do not discontinue bad habits, wrong people, negative thinking and poor decisions, it will destroy your dreams and future. Repeating the same mistakes and looking for different results is insanity and must be discontinued. Discontinue the unproductive, unprofitable, unnecessary things in your life and look for "God's new for you".

Thought for the Day:

New things come to replace the old. To make room, you must first let go.

Reflection

_____

_____

_____

_____

_____

_____

_____

_____

_____

_____

_____

_____

_____

_____

_____

_____

_____

_____

_____

_____

"For he shall give his angels charge over thee, to keep thee in all thy ways." Psalm 91:11 (KJV)

Divine Protection

In my home church, the elderly saints used to stand and testify to the goodness of the Lord. Quite frequently one mother would say, "I thank God for keeping me from seen and unseen danger." As a child, I thought that was ridiculous but, as I have grown older I realize the importance of God's protection over my life. There have been times that I have awakened late or got delayed going out of the house for work. On a number of these occasions I discovered that I if I had been a few minutes earlier, I could have been involved in an accident. The protection of God delayed me from catastrophe or early death. It is clearly amazing how God can be protecting all of His children simultaneously around the world but, that's the awesome God that we serve. God's protection allows us to arrive safely to our destination and fulfill our purpose.

God's shield of protection prohibits open, ambush attacks from the enemy who wants to destroy us before our time. Thank you God for your divine protection.

Challenge: Think back over your life of the many times that God has truly protected you. At your earliest convenience, testify to someone else of God's divine protection.

Thought for the Day:

Divine Protection is always there but, it is not designed for you to place yourself in harm's way.

Reflection

"Honest scales and balances belong to the LORD; all the weights in the bag are of his making."
Proverbs 16:11 (KJV)

Do Your Accounts Balance?

In the accounting field, there are several statements and/or reports that are run to let a business or a potential investor know the status of a company. The balance sheet indicates in detail if the company is profitable or has sustained a loss. Although, there is a profit/loss sheet, the balance sheet can tell the trained eye if a company is financially out of balance. Does the company have more liabilities than assets? Liabilities are expenses, losses from doing business, bad checks and non-profitable products and/or projects. Assets are items of income, acquiring equipment and the profit from good selling products or services. At the end of the balance sheet, the assets should equal liabilities and the accounts should balance. Some companies make the accounts balance. In most of the cases this is fraud or "cooking" the books.

They juggle the numbers to make them balance even though they have considerable liabilities and sustained monumental losses. Are you juggling the numbers or situations in your life to make life balance? People who spend a lot of time juggling are usually in denial. They don't want to face the fact that things are out of balance. Also, they don't want to make the changes necessary to bring balance. In the finance industry, you must be able to take a critical look at your financial situation to remain profitable. If something is out of balance, make changes. If you don't know what changes to make, seek professional help. Businesses do it all of the time. They seek financial consultants and advisors to help them make good business decisions. Do you need a life counselor to bring balance into your natural life? There is no shame in it and the New Year may be a good time to start. A recent interview with a financial advisor stated that one good thing that has come from the poor economy is that people are taking a hard look at their finances and making changes. Change is not always fun but, for abundant living, very necessary.

Spiritually, your life will always have more assets than liabilities because God is on your side. No matter how your life looks naturally, you will win in the end if you walk with God and obey His commands. Part of being able to live a balanced life, is to not carry unnecessary life liabilities on life's balance sheet. The scripture says lay aside every weight or sin that does so easily beset us Romans 12:1 (KJV). In business, profit is always money or assets, i.e. land, equipment, people and resources that can make you money. In your life, assets are not always money but, good health, peace of mind and surrounding yourself with people who genuinely love and want what's best for you. What's on your life's balance sheet? Are you in or out of balance? Don't just juggle the numbers or situations. Face the facts and make your life's accounts truly balance.

Challenge: Create your own balance sheet. List your life's assets and then list your life's liabilities. If there are more liabilities than assets, your life is out of balance. Where do you need to get your life back in balance? What liabilities do you need to remove?

Thought for the Day:

Balance your books before you are depleted of your resources and bankrupt your dreams. God's protection allows us to arrive safely to our destination and fulfill our purpose.

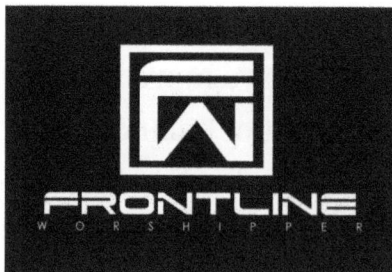

Reflection

_____

_____

_____

_____

_____

_____

_____

_____

_____

_____

_____

_____

_____

_____

_____

_____

_____

_____

_____

_____

_____

"Do you not know that in a race all the runners run, but only one gets the prize? Run in such a way as to get the prize." I Corinthians 9:24 (NIV)

Don't Quit, Stay in the Race

During the summer, the "Iron Man Louisville" race was held and thousands of participants, supporters, volunteers and organizers descended upon the city. Hotels were filled, streets were blocked off and security was on their post to make sure that nothing hindered the race from proceeding without incident. The volunteers were on hand to register the athletes, provide hospitality or direction and distribute water. But, more importantly they were there to encourage the participants in each event not to quit. Don't quit, keep going. As hard as the 2.4 mile swim, 112 mile bike ride and 26.4 mile run was for each person, the key to victory was to keep going and don't quit. The organizers and the city had done their part to make the race a success.

It was now up to each athlete to do their best. God has provided His best, Jesus Christ, the Holy Spirit, His power and His love to get us through anything in this life. If we walk in His way, He will clear the pathway for us to victory. Our job is to stay in this Christian Race and Don't Quit.

Thought of the Day:

In a race, winning is the goal but, finishing is a clear and amiable reality.

FRONTLINE
WORSHIPPER

<u>Reflection</u>

"And when he had called unto him his twelve disciples, he gave them power against unclean spirits, to cast them out, and to heal all manner of sickness and all manner of disease." Matthews 10:1 (KJV)

Don't Tear Up the Team

In collegiate sports, there are domineering teams that win championships multiple years. With seniors graduating and younger players entering the draft early, the likelihood of winning back to back championships is diminished greatly. Jesus was a coach par excellence. He picked his team, developed and mentored his team, blessed and sent them out on missions, corrected and rebuked their mistakes and even kept a hater on his team, Judas. Jesus' team was small but, effective. Even though Jesus was the expert and had all knowledge, He didn't tear up his team because of their inexperience or mistakes. He kept working with them because he knew their potential by the careers they were performing when he called them.

But, He also knew that with instruction and His father's power, they could spread the Gospel to the world. In the professional sports arena, some teams are dismantled and never reach championship level because of petty and personal preferential disagreements and disputes. Have you ever seen a runner-up team in a championship and given one more year they could have won it all? But, inevitably a player is traded or the coach is fired and they never seem to get that close again? Whether you have a supervisor on your job, coordinating a group of volunteers at church or in the community, coaching a little league team or parenting your team of children, don't tear up the team but:

See the Potential – Look beyond the current team member's ability and see what they can be with time.

Give them Experience – After you have given instruction, let them try out what they have learned. It might surprise you.

Correct Mistakes but, Praise Efforts – Praise effort even if the desired result isn't accomplished.

We all like to win but, when we don't, sometimes we won't even attempt to get back in the game if our efforts aren't acknowledged. Next it's time to fix what went wrong and teach them how to do it better next time.

Return to the Basics – When things don't work well in the game situation, you have to return to the basics. In baseball, you go to the batting cage. In basketball, you come early or stay late in practice and just shoot over and over again. In business, review the mission and vision statements then, brainstorm about sales strategies.

Bring in an outsider – Maybe your team is tired of you, the coach, and you need to bring in some fresh eyes, fresh mind and fresh ideas to review and refresh your team. You aren't the only one who does what you do. Look around, go to a conference or there are online resources that can help stimulate, motivate and revive your team.

Thought of the Day:

It takes a team to build a dream but, just one me to ensure defeat.

Reflection

"Enlarge the place of your tent, stretch your tent curtains wide, do not hold back; lengthen your cords, strengthen your stakes." Isaiah 54:2 (KJV)

Enlarged for More

Recently, Glad™ designed a new garbage bag made of stretchy more elastic material which enables the bag to hold more garbage. The marketing idea is if the garbage bag holds more you save money by buying fewer bags. The commercial showed the incredible and over exaggerated capacity of the bag to make their point. While looking at the commercial, I realized that we often don't reach our fullest potential because we are not prepared. Isaiah prophesied to Israel that God was about to bless them. He also told them that they needed to prepare themselves and their dwelling place for this large blessing. Since Israel lived in tents, the instructions were to enlarge the tent, stretch the curtains, lengthen the cords and strengthen the stakes.

Enlarge the tent – Broaden your scope of your dwelling. Get outside of your comfort zone. Enlarge your capacity to meet new people, explore new possibilities and experience new things.

Stretch the curtains –Stretch the curtains to allow the light of new enlightenment to shine through your dwelling. When you stretch the curtains, you can see out and others can see in. With enlightenment comes the exchange of resources, developing strategic partnerships and productive networking.

Lengthen the cords – The cords are your mind's ability to envision yourself going higher as well as bigger. Sometimes we talk and think too low therefore, our ability to rise above our circumstances remains on a low level. "For as he thinketh in his heart, so is he..." Proverbs 23:7 (KJV)

Strengthen the stakes – The stakes keep your tent held firmly on the ground. Build the tent or your life on a firm foundation, rooted and grounded in God, His word and His plan for your life.

Thought for the Day:

Pray to the Father for the ability to stretch your imagination to see yourself as He sees you.

Reflection

_____

_____

_____

_____

_____

_____

_____

_____

_____

_____

_____

_____

_____

_____

_____

_____

_____

_____

_____

_____

_____

"he did this only to teach warfare to the descendants of the Israelites who had not had previous battle experience." Judges 3:2 (NIV)

Experienced

When you are applying for a job, the person doing the interviewing is looking at several things. An interviewer examines how well you are dressed and your presentation, your qualifications and finally your experience. Even if you have presented yourself as a stellar employee and have the right qualifications, you may not be hired because of your lack of experience. Today, high school and college students are encouraged to have some experience working in their career field of choice even on a volunteer basis. Academic studies are wonderful and required but, there is nothing like having an employee with experience. This employee requires little job training and can be acclimated to the new particular company more quickly.

Additionally, the experienced employee is more productive and can help ease the work load in a department quickly. Do you know that God is looking to promote experienced warriors in His army? In Judges 3:2, God put the descendants of the Israelites into a battle to give them battle experience. They hadn't fought the wars with Joshua or King David. The children of Israel had more battles to fight but, they needed experience fighting, enduring and winning. People who have just become Christians are not placed in warfare situations until they are stronger and have more experience with the Lord. Over time the Lord will let you go through small skirmishes and battles with the enemy in order for you to get some experience. David said, I fought a lion and a bear and the Lord helped me to be victorious. His experience gave him courage to fight Goliath. Your troubles, trials and battles have not gone unnoticed by God. He saw you hang in there and withstand the attacks of the enemy. He gave you the power, strength and wisdom to endure.

He will reward you in due season but, the most important thing is that you can't get experience until you have had an experience. Ask the Savior to help you so that you can gain the experience you need to overcome! Use every opportunity presented to get the experience you need to excel and be victorious!

Thought of the Day:

Your work objective should be to gain the experience you need to do an even better job in the next assignment.

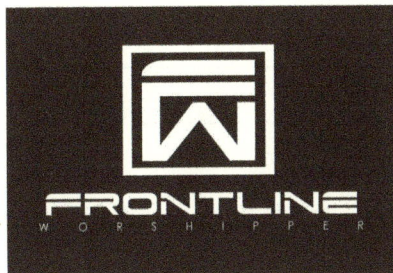

Reflection

_____

_____

_____

_____

_____

_____

_____

_____

_____

_____

_____

_____

_____

_____

_____

_____

_____

_____

_____

"Delight thyself also in the Lord and He shall give you the desires of your heart." Psalm 37:4 (KJV)

"Therefore I say unto you, What things soever ye desire, when ye pray, believe that ye receive them, and ye shall have them." Mark 11:24 (KJV)

Father Knows Best

While in the grocery store one day, I was at the self-checkout lane when there was a lot of screaming and crying at the back of the store. This was no normal sound of a child screaming. In fact, it was two children, in the same cart, screaming at the top of their lungs at their mother. The closer to the front of the store they got, the louder they screamed, begged and pleaded for her to buy what they wanted. The more they screamed the closer and faster she moved to the front door to exit. I paid for my food and I could still see and hear them screaming in the parking lot. The mother was on the phone and they realized it was their dad.

They tried to convince him to make their mother go back in the store to buy what they wanted. It was a mess to say the least. Back in the day, I would have received a whipping that I would still be talking about to this day. Today, you can't whip children in public. Child protective laws prevent such but, those children need a lot of discipline. I applaud the mom for maintaining her cool, continuing her quick pace out of the store and straight to the car. She didn't care how embarrassing or how noisy the scene she was not giving in to them. Have you ever pleaded, begged, cried, fasted, prayed, gave, bargained with and tried to convince God to give you something that you wanted? No matter how hard you tried, if it wasn't for you, it didn't happen. The two verses of scripture have been used in the context that whatever you want God will give it to you. But, in verse 3 of Psalm 37 and verse 22 of Mark 11, it says "trust in God" and "Have faith in God" respectively.

Why would you need faith in God if He is going to give you whatever you want anyway? Because when you trust and have faith in God, your trust and faith will be for what God wants for you and not just your lust for things. Trust in the Lord with all thine heart and lean not unto thy own understanding, in all thy ways acknowledge Him and He shall direct thy path. Proverbs 3:5-6 (KJV)

Earlier in my life I believed that God wanted me to marry a seemingly nice young man. He was Christian, devout, a deacon in his church and he was spiritual. He did not ask me to marry him after four years of dating. I prayed, fasted, cried, kept up my appearance and loved his family but, it didn't happen. After 3 dates with my husband I knew he wanted to marry me. God had chosen my husband for me all along. It was for me to keep moving forward until I met and fell in love with the person God wanted for me. No matter how long, loud and repetitious I was about wanting to marry someone else, God said no and I thank Him every day.

Those children in the grocery story may not get what they want for a very long time. They were trying to demand, embarrass and harass their mother into giving them what they wanted instead of what she wanted them to have. Fortunately, it didn't work. Your heavenly Father is no different. He has great things in store for you. He will bring them to you when you believe in Him, surrender your life and say, "God you know what's best for me."

Thought for the Day:

The father knows what's best for you. In the end, you will be glad you said "yes" to God's best.

FRONTLINE
WORSHIPPER

Reflection

_____

_____

_____

_____

_____

_____

_____

_____

_____

_____

_____

_____

_____

_____

_____

_____

_____

_____

"Therefore they will be like the morning mist, like the early dew that disappears, But I am the LORD your God, who brought you out of [b] Egypt. You shall acknowledge no God but me, no Savior except me."
Hosea 13:3-4 (KJV)

Fog

Several early mornings I have driven to work in the midst of thick fog. How does fog come into the atmosphere? A local meteorologist states that there are 3 reasons for fog, 1) cool temperatures 2) recent rainy weather and 3) no wind. Are you experiencing a season of fog in your life? In January, you were hot with excitement of the upcoming year and the opportunities, new projects and achievements that were yet to come. But, you found yourself face to face with the results of a cooling economy, cool reactions from people who didn't see your vision and ultimately, in October, your enthusiasm had cooled because of lack of support. Or maybe in January you had clear skies and the go ahead from your banker to invest money in the market.

Now your October investment statement indicates that you have suffered tumultuous rain of low market rates and substantial losses on your investment. Or maybe the winds of change didn't come to your house only to the White House. You licked your finger and placed it in the air and didn't feel the slightest hint of a breeze blowing new things in your life. This is called a season of fog. This season is only temporary. Hosea prophesied to the children of Israel that other gods would be like the morning mist or fog that would pass away. However, Jehovah, the true God who brought them out of Egypt was still their God. They should have no god but Him and there would be no Savior but Jehovah God. (Hosea 13:3-4) Fog disappears when the sun shines through the atmosphere. The season of problematic fog is temporary and will pass away with the light of the "Son" who will shine in your life. God's light will permeate any problem, situation or trouble in your life. Hold on and keep driving through the Season of Fog in your life.

Know that your spiritual fog will disappear when the Son shows up.

Thought for the Day:

Keep walking and moving on the journey of your life even when you can't see your way.

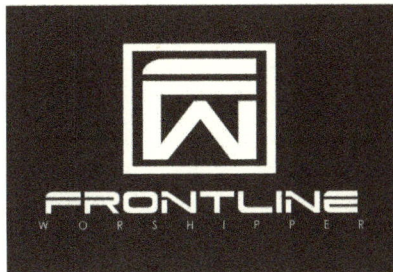

Reflection

"What is man that you make so much of him, that you give him so much attention...?" Job 7:17 (NIV)

"And many charged him that he should hold his peace: but he cried the more a great deal, Thou son of David, have mercy on me." Mark 10:48 (KJV)

Getting Your Attention

Babies at birth aren't able to speak words but, have a way of getting your attention. Babies cry, whimper, wave their arms and often just fidget. They may need to be changed, hungry or just want to be held but, they know how to get what they want and need. God gives us a communication system to get the attention we need to get our needs met. Even those who are born deaf can communicate through sign language. After we learn to speak, we can just tell people what we need or want. "Excuse me, would you pass me the salt and pepper." In Mark 10, there was a blind man who couldn't see Jesus but, heard that Jesus was passing by. He used his voice to get Jesus' attention so that he might receive his sight.

He yelled out "Thou son of David, have mercy on me." When that didn't work, he cried out louder until Jesus stopped and healed him. Job said, "what is man that you make so much of him and give him so much attention?" God is concerned about us and gives us attention when we need Him. In return, He wants our attention too. He wants us to pray to Him daily and not just when there is a problem. God has a way of getting our attention as well. That problem, situation or concern that you have is a way of getting your attention. God speaks through an audible voice, His word or another person to get your attention. How is God trying to get your attention right now? He's speaking, are you listening? No matter the method, God will get your attention to get His message to you. "Ladies and Gentleman, may I have your attention please?"

Thought of the Day:

Get the Father's attention any way you can but, always keep the Father's attention through your love, obedience and worship.

Reflection

"Then saith he to the man, Stretch forth thine hand..."
Matthew 12:13 (KJV)

Give Me Your Hand

Recently, while leaving the grocery store, I overheard a mother say to her child, "give me your hand." The child was too tall to be in the cart but, not quite tall enough to see to walk across the street by herself. The child and mother may have been to that grocery store many times, there still could have been an on-coming car or other danger that the child could not see. Are you walking and can't seem to see your way? Are you experiencing something unique that you need a guiding hand to walk you through? God says, "give me your hand." He is ready and willing to walk you across the street of an uncertain financial crisis, dysfunctional relationship or emotional meltdown. He sits high enough to see into your future. He can rearrange the affairs of your life to get you to your destiny. He asks that you "give me your hand."

If you want to go it alone and steer your own course, you place yourself in harm's way. You may be entering unchartered territory, experiencing unanticipated turbulence or you may be side swiped by an unforeseen circumstance. I am reminded of the old song, "walk with me lord, walk with me, while I'm on this tedious journey, I want Jesus to walk with me." But, let's change the words a little and say, "walk with you Lord, I want to walk with you." This is a strategic time and if you don't know where you are going, you can ask God to walk with you but, you need to be walking with Him. He said, "I am the way, the truth and life." Give Him your hand and let Him lead you perfectly to the promise.

Thought of the Day:

As long as the hand of God is guiding you it doesn't matter where you end up.

Reflection

"Each of you should give what you have decided in your heart to give, not reluctantly or under compulsion, for God loves a cheerful giver."
2 Corinthians 9:7 (KJV)

Giving: A Door to a Miracle

Giving has been a part of worship since biblical times. Offerings were given in the tabernacle. God has mandated man to give offerings of many kinds. Over time giving has been a dirty word in the church world. Some leaders have taken advantage of giving and become greedy. There will always be corruption while there is sin still in the world. Just because there is corruption does not negate the fact that God loves a cheerful giver. The Bible didn't say God loves a large amount giver but, a cheerful one. Whatever you have, give it cheerfully. Secondly, we see several instances in the Bible where people gave a small amount but, it was noticed or used greatly by Jesus. When the widow gave the two mites in the offering, Jesus took notice and said she had given more than any of them because she gave all she had.

When the little boy gave his two fish and five loaves of bread, Jesus took, blessed and broke it and performed the miracle of feeding at least five thousand. When God gave Jesus as the ultimate sacrifice for sin, all of humanity had the right to be forgiven of sin, access to God and eternal life. Oh, what a gift. Finally, giving is a door and not the only door to a miracle. There were several times in the Bible where people received a miracle and wanted to pay or give an offering. But the disciples refused it. They only asked that God be praised and tell others about what God had done in their lives. At times, I have been prompted by the Holy Spirit to give and nothing special happened but, I gave it as an act of obedience. Other times, I have been prompted to give and received an opportunity or benefit that wouldn't have happened otherwise. Giving is an act of your obedience. Trust God with what He has given you and offer to give it back to Him. What has God asked you to give? His tithe and our offerings are asked of each of us.

But what else has He placed in your heart to give? What are you holding on to that placed in God's hands will bless you and the world? Give and it shall be given to you pressed down, shaken together and running shall men heap into your bosom. Luke 6:38 (KJV)) Give and watch the door open to your miracle.

Thought of the Day:

Giving is an open door. Greed is an open door with a trap.

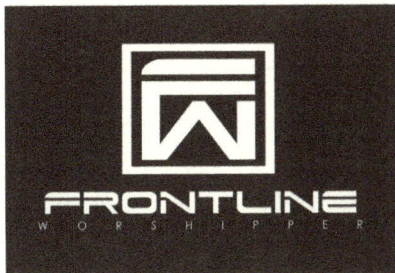

Reflection

_____

_____

_____

_____

_____

_____

_____

_____

_____

_____

_____

_____

_____

_____

_____

_____

_____

_____

"But I will stay on at Ephesus until Pentecost, because a great door for effective work has opened to me, and there are many who oppose me."
I Corinthians 16:8-9 (NIV)

"And pray for us, too, that God may open a door for our message..." Colossians 4:3 (NIV)

God's Open Door

In Corinthians 16, Paul states "a great door has opened unto me for effective work." This door that Paul refers to is an opportunity to share the message of Christ. There was much opposition to and persecution for preaching the message of Christ. In Colossians 4, Paul requests prayer for God to open a door for the message to be preached with clarity. Paul at that time, was in prison but, still had a desire to be effective in whatever opportunity came his way. Paul was prepared to share the message of Christ to the Colossians but, needed an opened door in order to be as effective as possible.

Recently, I was concerned about the doors that were not opening up to me. Then the Holy Spirit reminded me to be thankful for and maximize the doors of opportunity that were opened to me. Also, focus my efforts on being effective in the opened doors and don't concentrate on the unopened doors. A door is an opportunity but, can also be the receipt of grace or favor to complete a project, position or plan previously unavailable. Are there doors of opportunity opened in your life? Do you need a door opened? Pray that God will give you that open door. Secondly, prepare yourself for the door that is opened. Next, pursue that open door with all vigor. As did Paul, pray, prepare, pursue and praise God for the opportunity to share His mission, message or ministry. God said, "I have placed before you an open door that no one can shut". Revelations 3:8 (NIV)

Thought of the Day:

When opportunity is knocking, make sure you have one hand on the doorknob and the other hand in God's hand.

Reflection

"Now I know that the LORD is greater than all other gods...." Exodus 18:11 (NIV)

Greater Than or Less Than?

In elementary school, I had trouble with the greater than and less than math problems. I couldn't distinguish which number was greater or less by using this weird symbol. I knew my numbers in the correct order and the value of each. I knew that 5 was greater than or a larger number than 3 but, why was that variable in the middle to mess things up. My father worked with me tirelessly to get me to understand the concept. The symbol looked funny to me and didn't make any since. Even to this day after taking algebra II and trigonometry, I still have to look at the way the symbol is pointed before I can solve greater than or less than math problems. Are you trying to determine the value of certain things in your life? Have you determined that having a wonderful family may be greater than having a top notch career? Have you determined that pursuing your purpose is greater than pursuing people?

Have you determined that keeping up with the Jones' will make your life less than productive? What are the variables that you are using to draw your conclusion? Have you looked around and figured out that you are not greater than or less than anybody but, equal to the best you, you can be? Over the years, I have come to several conclusions, first, there is nothing greater than God so He is never entered into the greater than or less than or equal to equations. Second, I shouldn't compare myself to anybody when God's power is flowing through me and I am fulfilling His purpose for my life. Finally, my family is a part of the family of God and simply priceless. Complete your own life's equations and determine if it is greater than or less than the abundant life God has designed for you.

Thought of the Day:

God will always lead you to greater than you ever expected with less than the ability you had to offer.

Reflection

_____

_____

_____

_____

_____

_____

_____

_____

_____

_____

_____

_____

_____

_____

_____

_____

_____

_____

_____

"Guide me in your truth and teach me, for you are God my Savior, and my hope is in you all day long."
Psalm 25:5 (NIV)

"even there your hand will guide me, your right hand will hold me fast." Psalm 139:10 (NIV)

The Great Guidance Counselor

A good guidance counselor is essential when navigating the academic waters in high school and especially college. A well mapped out course schedule or plan will eliminate unnecessary courses and concentrate on those courses that are critical to the goal of a diploma or degree. Although guidance counselors are not perfect, if the plan is followed and the courses are passed successfully, you will have the degree. I can attest to the fact that having a guidance counselor has helped me significantly. Years prior to meeting my husband, I was guided by the Holy Spirit to make some changes in my life to prepare for my future. I did not know these changes would be the key to marrying my husband.

Had I not changed, I might still be single or not prepared for the man that God intended for me.

I believe that the Holy Bible is our ultimate spiritual guidance counselor. But, God through His Spirit can give us individual specific instructions that help us to live our life's destiny and purpose. Our Salvation is secured through Jesus Christ but, living the abundant life is obtained through obedience and submission to God's will for our lives. Are you listening to the guidance counselor for your life? Are you emulating someone else's life and making it your own? What does God want to do through you? No matter how uncomfortable or slight the change may be it could be the key to reaching your destiny. The ultimate goal is not to live an adequate life but, the abundant life. Abundant living does not mean wealth, fame or fortune for everyone but abundant living is living the life that God has intended for you no matter the occupation.

Whether you are a lawyer or a live-in nanny or a doctor or a doorman or a mother or a missionary, live your life by God's guidance and for His glory.

Thought of the Day:

God will guide you with eternal, not just long term, goals in mind.

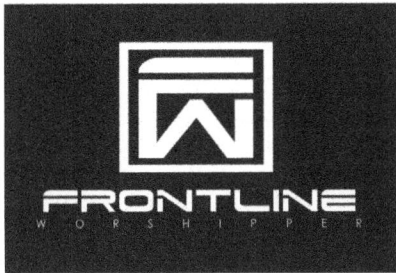

FRONTLINE
WORSHIPPER

Reflection

_____

_____

_____

_____

_____

_____

_____

_____

_____

_____

_____

_____

_____

_____

_____

_____

_____

_____

_____

_____

"...because the LORD brought you out of it with a mighty hand.." Exodus 13:3 (NIV)

"...and hath kept his servant from evil..."
I Samuel 25:39 (KJV)

He Brought Us, He Kept Us

My home church choir used to sing a song, "look how far he brought us from, look how God brought us from, He has kept us day by day, look how far the Lord has brought us from". The vamp of the song just simply said, "he brought us, he kept us". I can still here that vamp repeated over and over again. We sang it until we believed it. We sang it until we re-membered and began to thank Him. We sang it until others got happy about it too. I challenge you today to look back over the past twelve months and see how far God has brought you. Think about the many good and bad situations He brought you through. Thank and praise Him for the many hills, mountains, valleys and tragedies. More importantly, thank and praise Him for keeping you through it all.

Thank Him for keeping you in your right mind when you thought you were going to lose it. Thank Him for keeping your family safe and sound from, "seen and unseen" dangers, as the seasoned saints used to say. Thank Him for keeping you with a "reasonable portion of health and strength" as the deacons used to pray. Another old song comes to mind that says, "Jesus you brought me all the way, and you carry my burdens every day, oh you're such a wonderful savior, I've never known you to fail me, you brought me thank God, all of the way." Truly He brought us and kept us all the way until this present moment in time.

Challenge: Get a piece of paper and write down all of the major events that God brought you through in the past 12 months. Count your blessings and watch God multiply them.

Thought for the Day:

Count your blessings they will always outnumber your worries, cares and bills.

Reflection

"To see thy power and thy glory, so as I have seen thee in the sanctuary." Psalm 63:2 (KJV)

"Whither shall I go from thy spirit? or whither shall I flee from thy presence?" Psalm 139:7 (KJV)

Hide and Seek

Ever played hide and seek and the person could hide very well? The usual places to hide would be empty and you had to look and look. After so long, you just gave up and yelled, "come out, come out, where ever you are." But, even then, they didn't come out and you eventually found them in the house. The house was not on the hiding list but, there they are sitting in front of the TV or asleep on the couch. Hot, frustrated and angry you begin to fuss because you searched but, couldn't find them. Does it seem like God is hiding from you? Even though He promised never to leave or forsake you, do you feel forsaken? In Psalm 139, David remembered there was no hiding from God's presence. God is a spirit. God's Spirit is everywhere and knows everything.

You cannot play hide and seek from God. Even though you may feel abandoned or it seems God has left you, your feelings can be deceiving. God promised never to leave you and He won't. He is right there with you all the time. He is in the house, waiting on you. You are the temple of the Holy Spirit. You are the dwelling place. He is residing in you and not hiding at all. There is no need for hide and seek, God is not hiding He is just resting.

Thought of the Day:

God is not hiding as much as He is wanting to be sought after.

Reflection

_____

_____

_____

_____

_____

_____

_____

_____

_____

_____

_____

_____

_____

_____

_____

_____

_____

_____

_____

"Jesus refused..." Luke 9:60 (The Message)

I Didn't Order This

Have you ever been in a restaurant and placed your order but, suddenly another server arrives at your table with an order you didn't place? I have. The food looked great on the plate and probably would have tasted good too but, that wasn't what I ordered. On the occasions that this has happened to me, as soon as they placed it before me, I realized that it is not mine. I didn't touch the plate, cut into it or even breathe on the food because it was not mine. That food was ordered by someone else. It was theirs. Why is it we stay in relationships, keep pursuing projects and accept assignments that we know are not ours or that we didn't or shouldn't have ordered? Once I was in a relationship and realized that this was not the life I was designed to lead, I left. Yes, it hurt. Yes, I cried. Yes, I felt sad, mad and relieved all at the same time but, it wasn't what I ordered.

This was not the relationship that was designed for me. You might say that rejecting someone else's food is easy but, leaving a relationship is much harder. True but, are you going to stay in an abusive relationship or situation because you are too embarrassed to leave? Admit, I didn't sign up for or order this, I must go now. On the other hand, there are some things that I didn't order that just came in my life. These things were out of my control and it just happened. This is possible too but, it is here now so it is now in your control as to what happens next. You can reject it or accept it. It is your choice and left up to you what you tolerate in all areas of your life and not just food service. You can reject the delivery of unordered, undesired and unnecessary things to you. Just say, "no, I didn't order that." Just say, "no, I didn't agree to this". Just say, "no, I will not sign that contract". If you didn't order it, say "no." Otherwise, you could continue to accept things that may hurt you, may devastate you emotionally and destroy your future. Say it along with me, "I'm sorry, I didn't order this."

Thought of the Day:

If your order is not correct, send it back immediately. Don't waste time or energy on what is not ordered for your life.

Reflection

"Hear counsel, and receive instruction, that thou mayest be wise in thy latter end." Proverbs 19:20 (KJV)

Instructed for the Best

Recently, I watched two model reality shows. One is Tyra Banks' "America's Next Top Model" and the other is Tyson Beckford's "Make me into a Supermodel." I have no interest in modeling or ever wanting to be a model. But, there are several commonalities on both of these shows. 1) all of the contestants stand on the threshold and brink of their ultimate goal, 2) the contestants have been introduced to people who are at the top of the fashion/modeling industry 3) the producers of the show have invested time, money and advise, free food, housing and clothing. In addition, they have access to the top make-up artists, hair stylists, photographers, etc. who continually tell each contestant, "we want what's best for you and your career." As the competition progresses, the one thing that separates the men from the boys and the women from the girls is the ability to take constructive criticism or instruction and become better.

The episode I watched had a beautiful young woman that was eventually, eliminated because she wouldn't follow instructions and it came out in her pictures. She kept saying over and over, "but, I know I'm the prettiest girl here." Being the prettiest girl meant nothing when it came time to produce the picture or complete the challenge asked of them. We all have egos that love to be stroked. Feeling sorry for ourselves and not working through difficulties will not help you get better, only worse. God has a great plan for your life. He desires to give you his best and knows what is best for you. His best is so great that if He doesn't prepare you for it, you will waste, lose, mishandle or destroy it. Follow the instructions. Go through the process. In the end, God will bring His best out of you.

Thought of the Day:

The teachable will always get better. Those unwilling to be taught will be embarrassed.

<u>Reflection</u>

_____

_____

_____

_____

_____

_____

_____

_____

_____

_____

_____

_____

_____

_____

_____

_____

_____

_____

_____

"He gave His only begotten son...." John 3:16 (KJV)

Irreplaceable Gift

My husband bought me a practical and pricey Christmas gift. The present was a Bose speaker system that would allow me to play my background tracks via iPod for music ministry. I was thrilled with the gift. It is portable. It gives out great sound. I had no more skipping tracks with a CD player.   As much as I love this gift, over time and with the advancement of technology, there will be something that will replace this system. It will be more portable. It will produce a better sound. It may or may not cost more but, this system can and will be replaced. Jesus was and is an irreplaceable gift from God to the world. He stands alone as the only irreplaceable person and relationship in your life. He is the only way to eternal life. No matter how close you are to family and friends, Jesus is the true irreplaceable gift.

There will not be another coming after Him. He will not be upgraded, updated, revised or recalled. He is truly one of a kind. The sad thing is that people reject this irreplaceable gift every day just as they did in ancient times. That doesn't make Jesus any less viable, important, necessary or irreplaceable. If you don't know Him, accept the gift of Jesus' love today. If you know Him, appreciate Him more every day. Let Him know daily that He is the irreplaceable gift in your life.

Thought of the Day:

Irreplaceable gifts are to be cherished. Replaceable gifts will be discarded.

Reflection

"Now when Jesus was risen early the first day of the week, he appeared first to Mary Magdalene, out of whom he had cast seven devils. And she went and told them that had been with him, as they mourned and wept. And they, when they had heard that he was alive, and had been seen of her, believed not. After that he appeared in another form unto two of them, as they walked, and went into the country."
Mark 16:9-12 (The Message)

Jesus is Alive, In Another Form!

Recently, I purchased a cleaning product in a liquid form instead of the powder. While cleaning the bathroom with the powder form and spreading it everywhere, I remembered that I had the same brand, same type of cleaner but, in a liquid form. When I picked up the liquid, I was surprised at the lack of mess, direct aim of the solution and the quicker clean up. This new liquid formula helped me to clean easier and better. What if I was unwilling to try something new? This product was from the same company, same product and the same name but, in a different form.

God is multi-faceted and there are multiple names for God because He can do so many different things. He is always God but, He can be a lamb as easy as a lion. In Mark 6, this is just after Jesus was resurrected triumphant from the Grave. He appeared unto Mary in one form in the Garden. But, later Jesus appeared unto two unnamed people in another form in the country. In both instances, when Mary Magdelene and the two unnamed people told that they had seen the risen Jesus, people didn't believe it. They had seen Jesus crucified but, didn't believe that He could really be raised from the dead. Some people miss God because they expect him to come in the same way every time. Jesus rose from the grave but, He sent His Spirit to live inside each of us. The Holy Spirit can appear in many forms and work through many people. Each day when you wake up, expect God to show up in your life. He may not take the same form each day but, expect a powerful impact to be demonstrated in your life.

Thought of the Day:

Help me to always see God throughout my day. Help me to also be one of the people He uses to bless someone else.

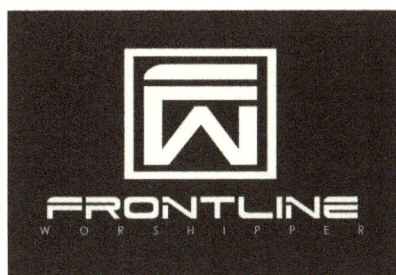

Reflection

_____

_____

_____

_____

_____

_____

_____

_____

_____

_____

_____

_____

_____

_____

_____

_____

_____

_____

_____

"For whosoever will save his life shall lose it; but whosoever shall lose his life for my sake and the gospel's, the same shall save it." Mark 8:35 (KJV)

Just Surrender

If you are an action movie fan like me, you have heard many times the phrases, "this is the police, you are surrounded, come out with your hands up." If the criminals follow instructions and come out with their hands up and have no weapon, there shouldn't be any trouble, shooting or death. But, you always have that one criminal in the movie that they have to chase and possibly shoot because he won't surrender. The chase is through yards, over fences, dodging the elderly and screaming women with children just to catch the criminal. All the while the police officer is yelling, "stop, freeze!" Now you may not be a criminal or ever committed a crime but, God has surrounded you with His love and power. He is not going to chase you but, He will stand with arms outstretched and wait for you to come to Him.

He asks that you surrender. He surrounds you with His peace to take you through every storm. He surrounds you with His protection from the enemies in this world. Come to Him with your hands up, white flag waving and yell, "don't shoot any more love darts at me, I surrender." If you surrender your life to Him, He will give you the best life here on earth and eternal life with Him in heaven. Just Surrender....

Thought of the Day:

Surrendering with God isn't giving up, it is free falling into the arms of safety.

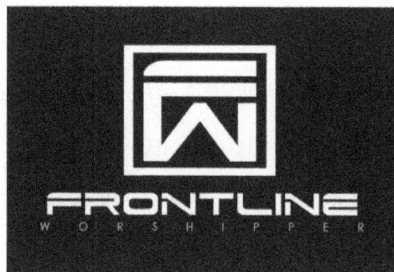

Reflection

_____

_____

_____

_____

_____

_____

_____

_____

_____

_____

_____

_____

_____

_____

_____

_____

_____

_____

_____

"...to make ready a people.." Luke 1:17(KJV)

"....to equip his people for works of service, so that the body of Christ may be built up." Ephesians 4:12 (NIV)

Make Ready a People

We are approaching the end of summer. Teachers, students, parents and department stores are getting ready for the start of school. School is the preparation center for a community, state or nation for students to become viably skilled to contribute to our global society. The job of teachers is to make ready a generation with the necessary skills and tools to be productive citizens. In Luke, it was foretold that John the Baptist's role would be to prepare or make ready the children of Israel for the Messiah. In Ephesians 4, Paul was writing to the church at Ephesus encouraging the members there to work in harmony with the gifts they had been given to prepare God's people for the work of the ministry and to build up the body of Christ.

He told them that some may be pastors, teachers or prophets but, the goal of the gift is to teach and strengthen the body of believers to be productive citizens in the Heavenly Kingdom. The Kingdom of God is at hand, what are you doing to make ready a people for His return? Are you using your God given gift to make ready the next generation for Kingdom building? Christ is coming back soon. Whether you are a preacher, teacher, usher, greeter, singer or other volunteer, when Christ returns will He find your post giving 100%? As tens of thousands of schools reopen, reopen you heart, ears and mind to obtain direction from God for your role in making ready a people. The time is now to make ready a people trained in spiritual warfare to demolish the enemies' kingdom and build up and recruit hard for God's Kingdom

Thought of the Day:

Are You Ready?

Reflection

"These are the men David put in charge of the music in the house of the LORD after the ark came to rest there."
1 Chronicles 6:31 (NIV)

Making His Band

The MTV reality series, *"Making His Band"* has attracted some extremely naturally gifted musicians. Those singers and musicians selected in the first round to live in the house are now having their skills challenged with difficult sheet music. Two of the musicians do not read music and they are struggling. Additionally, one musician as a youngster was told by a family member to learn to read music and he didn't do it. The music to be learned is hard on its own even if you do read music but, what if sheet music is a foreign language and you have three days to learn it? What do you do?

+ Quit and go home

+ Work night and day to learn the music

+ Ask for help and do your best.

I pick answers 2 and 3. Quitting and going home is not an option for me. If you have an opportunity to do a job, help on a committee, display your gifts or bake a cake give it 1000% and with excellence. "And David danced before the LORD with all his might;..." 2 Samuel 6:14 (KJV). David danced with everything that was within him. Are you giving the task your all? Secondly, sometimes you have to ask for help. "....Lord, save me" Matthew 14:30 (KJV) Peter was drowning and he asked Jesus to save him. In other words, Peter was in the water over his head and asked for help. Have you have found yourself in a situation over your head and were too embarrassed to ask for help? You feel like you are drowning but, the good news is, ask and you shall receive help. In any difficult situations or hard tasks, give it your all but, when it's too much, ask for help.

Challenge: How do you handle difficult situations when you are not fully prepared for the task? How did it turn out? In the future, how do you think that you could handle them better?

Thought of the Day:

Weight lifting builds muscle in the body. Difficulties by prayer and seeking God will build spiritual muscles.

FRONTLINE
WORSHIPPER

Reflection

"A double minded man is unstable in all of his ways."
James 1:8 (KJV)

Out of Balance

I recently cooked some brownies in a convection oven. Convection ovens double as a traditional oven and microwave. One problem with cooking in this type of oven is that the container that you are cooking with must fit on the metal or glass revolving tray. Secondly, the oven cooks a lot hotter even on the traditional oven setting because of the microwave oven capability. I cooked the brownies but, the weight of the pan shifted while in circular motion. When I took them out of the convection oven one third of the pan was over cooked and almost burned up. Two thirds of the brownies in the pan were still raw but, the one third of the brownies in the middle was actually done and edible. Do you ever feel like only a third of your life is producing great results? One third of your life is overworked to death, one third of your life is still raw and undeveloped but, the other third of your life is running smoothly. How do you bring your life into proper alignment and balance? By standing on the only firm, level and peaceful foundation, Jesus Christ. My brownies would have turned out better if I had set them on a regular, even and balanced cooking rack in a regular oven. Your life will be productive, satisfying and peaceful if you turn your life over to Jesus Christ. Jesus Christ is the rock and the sure, firm foundation to place your life. When you are tempted to get out of balance, He will give you the power to stabilize you and get you back in balance. With the proper balance and alignment, you will complete your assignment, enjoy people and live the abundant life. If you are out of balance or unstable, put your faith and trust in Jesus today. Jesus can bring your life into balance in a most phenomenal way.

Thought of the Day:

Make up your mind, balance your life and journey with God in peace.

Reflection

_____

_____

_____

_____

_____

_____

_____

_____

_____

_____

_____

_____

_____

_____

_____

_____

_____

_____

_____

"And it shall come to pass, while my glory passeth by, that I will put thee in a clift of the rock, and will cover thee with my hand while I pass by." Exodus 33:22 (KJV)

"Insomuch that they brought forth the sick into the streets, and laid them on beds and couches, that at the least the shadow of Peter passing by might overshadow some of them." Acts 5:15 (KJV)

Pass by me

In the two passages of scripture given, there were miraculous things that happened while passing by. In Exodus, God was passing by Moses to show him His glory from the back because no man can look directly at God and live. God had such a relationship with Moses that He trusted Moses with showing His glory while He passed by. After this point, Moses wrote the history of the world in Genesis and we now have the record of the glory of creation. In Acts, because of the relationship that Peter had with God, sick people were able to be healed simply by Peter's shadow. Wow! What a gift from an awesome God!

The power was not because of Peter but, because of the God in Peter. What do people experience when they pass by you? Do you impart encouragement or discouragement? Do people look at you and can't explain what it is but, they are drawn to you? Or is your mere passing unpleasant and people don't desire to be in your company? Oh to experience the glory, presence and healing power of God while He passes by me. Anytime, anywhere and any place, pass by me....

Thought of the Day:

The closer you get to God the more He will reveal Himself to you. Stay close.

Reflection

"Furthermore then we beseech you, brethren, and exhort you by the Lord Jesus, that as ye have received of us how ye ought to walk and to please God, so ye would abound more and more."
I Thessalonians 4:1 (KJV)

"By faith Enoch was translated that he should not see death; and was not found, because God had translated him: for before his translation he had this testimony, that he pleased God." Hebrews 11:5 (KJV)

Please God

God placed in each of us an innate desire to please. First, we wanted to please our parents. Then we sought to please our teachers, coaches, spouses, children and friends. There are many of us today who only seek to please ourselves. What a self-absorbed and unfulfilled way to live! But, if we seek to please God, there are so many benefits that we enjoy and experience with others. If we allow the love of God to flow through us, we can share this love with others through service and with compassion. Also, God's power and grace will be upon us to forgive, rebuild and restore relationships.

Additionally, He will give us the power to fulfill His purpose and destiny for our lives. The ultimate fulfillment in life is to be used of God for His glory and His good pleasure. Who wouldn't want to please God? God is the creator and giver of all things. Secondly, we will one day face Him to give an account of what we did with our lives, gifts and His son, Jesus Christ. Will He be pleased with how you have spent your life on earth or will He be frowning? My desire is to hear Him say, "Well done my good and faithful servant." What about you?

Thought of the Day:

If you seek to please God, He will be pleased with you. If you seek to please others, misery will overshadow you.

FRONTLINE
WORSHIPPER

Reflection

_____

_____

_____

_____

_____

_____

_____

_____

_____

_____

_____

_____

_____

_____

_____

_____

_____

_____

_____

_____

"And thine ears shall hear a word behind thee, saying, This is the way, walk ye in it.." Isaiah 30:21 (KJV)

Power from Behind

Isn't it amazing that the rearview mirror in your car is so small? Positioned in the middle of the front window, this accessory will enable you to see what's behind you as well as what's in front. Why do you need to see what's behind you? Isn't the most important thing going forward? Going forward is important but, there can be lessons learned and equipping power gained from looking behind. For example,

Parking. Sometimes you need to stop driving and park. Parking will allow you time to regroup, recover and rethink your next destination. But, to avoid an accident, you need to check your rearview mirror to make sure that you can park safely and securely. In all thy ways acknowledge him and he shall direct thy path. Proverbs 3:6 (KJV)

Passing. The rearview mirror allows you to see clearly and safely before you pass into another lane of traffic. The ability to pass will give us the right of way to stay on the right course. Teach me thy way, O LORD, and lead me in a plain path, because of mine enemies. Psalm 27:11 (KJV)

Potential to block others. The rearview mirror will allow you to get out the way of speeding cars, emergency vehicles or police who are moving quickly to assist others in need. "He has blocked my way so I cannot pass;..." Job 19:8 (KJV) Although you want to arrive at your destination safely, you also don't want to block someone else from getting to their destination.

Pull over to obtain help. If you have a stalled vehicle or flat tire, an emergency lane allows you to pull over and obtain help. "Send thee help from the sanctuary..." Psalm 20:2 (KJV) Take courage in knowing that staying in the emergency lane is only temporary and that help is on the way.

Praise for safe passage. From the rearview mirror, you can see how far God has brought you and give Him praise for safe passage. "And thou shalt be secure, because there is hope; ... and thou shalt take thy rest in safety." Job 11:18 (KJV)

The rearview mirror is a small accessory in a car but, gives us knowledge and power to reach our destination. Don't take for granted the ability to look in your rearview mirror and know that there is power from looking behind.

Thought of the Day:

Goodness and mercy shall follow you and blessings will overtake you. Turn around it just could be coming from behind.

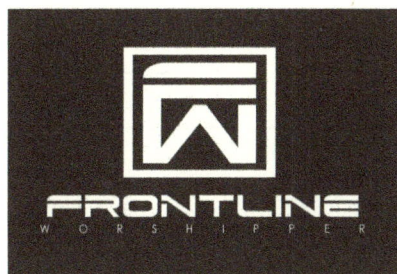

Reflection

"He is despised and rejected of men; a man of sorrows.." Isaiah 53:3 (KJV)

"He came unto his own, and his own received him not." John 1:11 (KJV)

Power of Rejection

Rejection is hard for any of us to receive. Our innate desire is to be accepted for who we are and what we do. Each day we strive to put our best foot forward and bring our "A" game to any situation. But, sometimes you are rejected. Rejection can come on purpose or by accident. At some point in life we all will experience rejection on one level or another. How do you handle rejection? Are your feelings hurt? Do you want to give up when rejected? Whether you want to admit it or not, we have all had these emotions and more, following rejection. But, how can you look at rejection as a positive instead of negative? I am glad that you asked.

Some new thoughts about rejection are:

Redirection – focus your efforts on the places, people and projects that are accepting you and your ideas. In other words, go where they want you. If a God opportunity is knocking and beating down your door in some area of your life, open the door wide and welcome it.

Restructure-conduct an evaluation of the project, process or proposal that was rejected. Do you need to tweak some things and then resubmit the same idea to another organization? Is there a person that needs to be eliminated from or added to the committee to make the idea or project accepted? Review, pray, restructure and then resubmit and see if the project is accepted or not.

Rejuvenation-Don't retreat but, renew your efforts. Each rejection should add fuel to the fire of determination to press forward and succeed. The trick of the enemy is to discourage you and make you stop but, when rejection comes you should renew your efforts all the more.

Rejoice-Jesus told His disciples to rejoice when men reject, hate and exclude you for great is your reward in heaven. "Blessed are you when men hate you, when they exclude you and insult you and reject your name as evil, because of the Son of Man. "Rejoice in that day and leap for joy, because great is your reward in heaven. For that is how their fathers treated the prophets." Luke 6:22-23 (NIV)

Jesus told his disciples that if they don't receive you, shake the dust off your feet and keep right on going. "The very dust, in the day of judgment, will rise up and be a testimony." (Luke 9:5 NIV) When you are rejected, redirect, restructure, rejuvenate your efforts and rejoice to your heavenly father for He will give you the power to overcome rejection.

Thought of the Day:

Rejection from men is fuel for promotion from God.

Reflection

_____

_____

_____

_____

_____

_____

_____

_____

_____

_____

_____

_____

_____

_____

_____

_____

_____

_____

_____

"Jeremiah said, "God's Message came to me like this: Prepare yourself!" Jeremiah 32:6 (The Message)

"Moreover, brethren, I would not that ye should be ignorant..." I Corinthians 10:1 (KJV)

Prepare Yourself

When it's time to go back to school the stores are filled with school supplies. There are large bins, up front and clearly marked for easy access to meet the needs of the upcoming school year. The "Back to School" commercials are in full swing on television. In my community, the schools provide the larger stores with their school supply lists so the parents have no excuse. The parents are dancing in the aisles and smiling all the way to the checkout cashier. The kids have been home for 2 ½ months and it is now time for them to go back to school. Hallelujah, Praise the Lord, we are all getting back on a regular schedule. By law, children have to be educated, trained and prepared.

After you turn 18, there is no law that states that you have to go to college, trade school or even take a free class at a community center or church. From teachers to hair stylists to doctors and lawyers, you are required to attend hours of professional development to retain your license or certification. Look at the status of your life; is there an area that needs to be developed, information obtained or skills revised? Are you adequately prepared for the career in the industry where you are employed? Whether you go back to college, trade school or not, prepared yourself by:

Reading as much as possible. The public library is free, you pay for it with your tax dollars. Those manuals, handouts and online programs that were referenced in your job orientation or community training, go back and read them.

Community Events. Attending a church or nonprofit or community outreach event that provides access to information about social, economic and health issues. It's free!

Workshops. Offering to attend workshops, conferences and training sessions paid for by your company with a topic that is in-directly related to your department but, directly related to your industry.

Network. Get the business cards of the instructors at the conferences or workshops that you attend. Email them back, go to their website, buy their books and find out as much as possible.

In the King James Version of the Bible, the word "prepare" or an extension of that word is mentioned 182 times. Even God wanted people, places and things prepared in specific ways for His service. God wants you to be as prepared as possible in every area of your life. God gave you His Word which you can study and know His ways. God gave you His Spirit to empower you to do what He requires. God gave you Himself in Jesus Christ as the proof that He loves you and wants what's best for you.

What else do you need? Get up, get moving and know that it's time to prepare yourself for the next level of abundant living. God Bless You!

Thought for the Day:

Preparation is never time wasted but, time well invested.

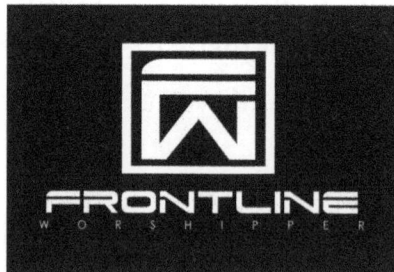

Reflection

_____

_____

_____

_____

_____

_____

_____

_____

_____

_____

_____

_____

_____

_____

_____

_____

_____

_____

_____

_____

"For promotion cometh neither from the east, nor from the west, nor from the south. But God is the judge: he putteth down one, and setteth up another."
Psalm 75:6-7 (KJV)

Promotion Assured

Prior to David assuming the promotion and position of King, he had to endure many things. First, after he was anointed King, he had to return to his first job of keeping sheep. Have you ever been told that you were going to get a promotion but, it was delayed? Be patient because delayed does not mean denied, just postponed. Remain consistent in your current role/job/career because that is what qualified you for the promotion. Secondly, David's gift brought him one step closer to his promotion because he became the chief musician for King Saul. This was a good thing. But, King Saul became jealous of David after he killed Goliath. This was now a bad thing because Saul desired to kill David. Thus, David was pursued and aggravated by Saul's hatred until Saul's death. This was another postponement but, God's Word will stand forever.

Thirdly, David found a partner who would help propel him to the next level, Jonathan, King Saul's son. Jonathan knew that David was to be King even though he, himself was next in line. Oh the blessing of understanding your role and position. In the end, David rose to power as King of all Israel but, not without his problems. Like King David, do you see yourself in one of these stages of promotion?

Promotion by Anointing - You may have been anointed or chosen for the promotion but, experience a delay. The promotion may be delayed but, not denied, so hold on.

Problems upon Acceptance – You may have accepted the promotion or position but, find that instead of enjoying it, the problems have just begun.

Pursued and Aggravated – Jealousy will make your enemies pursue and aggravate you to give up your position but, hold on.

Postponement of Acceptance – Saul knew that David was the next king but, he refused to accept it. Some people will deny that you have the position but, just because they don't accept it doesn't make it not come to past. This attitude is just a postponement of the inevitable.

Propel to Achievement – There are people that God will bring into your life to propel you to your achievement. These people are mature enough to speak into your life and provide the resources to assist you.

Powerful Accomplishment – In the end, no matter what gift or talent you have, it will be God who will get the glory for each and every accomplishment.

If you walk with God, there will be times of humility, celebration, aggravation and promotion. Know that God is able to keep you and carry you through to the end.

Promotion from man may alter with each emotion and/or whim but, promotion from God is assured.

Thought of the Day:

Promotion comes to the prepared, positioned and prayerful.

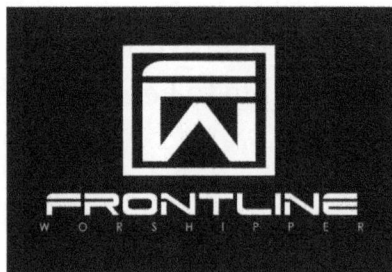

Reflection

"After these things the LORD appointed other seventy also, and sent them two and two before his face into every city and place, whither he himself would come."
Luke 10:1 (KJV)

Puzzle Piece in the Wrong Place?

Have you ever worked a puzzle and put a piece of the puzzle in the wrong place? It looked like it would fit. It was similar to the shape you needed. The color of the puzzle was the same but it didn't fit perfectly. You have assembled a great team of gifted and qualified people but, they are in the wrong place. On their resumes, it looked like all the parts of your team puzzle would fit together but, it doesn't. Put the resumes down and look at the people for a moment. Are you trying to fit an introvert where an extrovert should be placed? Are you trying to position a person who is a great team member as the leader? Are you trying to promote someone based on their loyalty but, if promoted, would destroy themselves and the department?

Realize as a coach that you can't base every decision on your personal likes and dislikes. What asset does the team member bring to help achieve the vision of the organization? Will the leader you choose, allow others to learn, develop and grow? Building a team is an important and critical undertaking. As with a puzzle, after you assemble the pieces together, there still may be one person in the wrong place. Don't hesitate to remove or replace that person with the better fit. It is hard but, it is essential to having the vision fulfilled and not pampering personalities. If there is a piece of your team puzzle in the wrong place? Fix it.

Thought of the Day:

Puzzles are only complete when all of the pieces are in the right place.

Reflection

"As a dog returns to its vomit, so a fool repeats his folly." Proverbs 26:11 (NIV)

"And whosoever will not receive you, when ye go out of that city, shake off the very dust from your feet for a testimony against them." Luke 9:5 (KJV)

Repeats

In Proverbs, the teacher states that as a dog returns to its vomit, so a fool repeats his folly. Are you repeating the same mistakes over and over again? Do you find yourself regurgitating the mess of your past and then ultimately repeating it? Then commit today to have "no more repeats." Human beings are created to have a higher intellectual and mental capacity than animals but, to prove it you need to do it. Stop falling for the same empty promises from manipulative people. Stop giving some people your best love, time and money only to have that effort stomped on or not reciprocated. You are not a fool but, one of God's greatest creations. Act like it! In Luke, when Jesus sent out his disciples to spread the gospel, He gave them specific instructions.

But, He also said, if people do not receive you or my gospel, when you leave and shake the dust off your feet. The very dust will be a testimony on the Day of Judgment against them. Don't repeat the mistakes of your past. Be cordial but, eliminate people from your inner circle that repeatedly disappoint or hurt you. More importantly, realize that the approval of God is more important than the approval of certain men. Shake the dust off your feet and keep moving forward. Look at your life and determine, what do I keep repeating? I encourage you to repeat the following:

Repeat seeking God for His divine direction and quickly obey

Repeat that God created you in His image and that He has divine purpose for your life

Repeat that God has great things in store but, you must walk and wait for His divine timing.

Repeat relationships with quality people that live a healthy, positive and Christian lifestyle

Repeat over and over again God's word to empower abundant living.

Challenge: List three people, situations or habits that you have repeated within the past year that were not beneficial to your life. Ask yourself honestly, why? Then, pray for guidance and a commitment to stop repeating these same actions. Then determine a list of quality actions, people or situations that you will repeat in the upcoming month and year.

Thought of the Day:

Repeat God's promises, repeat God's purpose but, repent of the unnecessary.

Reflection

_____

_____

_____

_____

_____

_____

_____

_____

_____

_____

_____

_____

_____

_____

_____

_____

_____

_____

_____

"...that I have set before you life and death, blessing and cursing: therefore choose life...."
Deuteronomy 30:19 (KJV)

Resurrect it or Bury It!

One of the critical components of our daily lives is decision making. Whether you are a business owner, home maker or in ministry, you have to make critical decisions that will affect the direction and quality of your daily life. In this delicate economy, you must be as strategic as possible regarding how your time, your energy and especially, how your money is spent. You cannot just contribute to the same projects or same organizations just because you always have in the past. Evaluate their effectiveness. Determine if they are good stewards of the treasures that they have been given. Is this critical to my God-given purpose or should I be putting my efforts somewhere else? Decide whether you should resurrect it or bury it.

Jesus was buried in a borrowed tomb but, He declared long before he was crucified that He would be resurrected in three days. Jesus had been given all power to be resurrected. We have all been given the power of free will. We can, with God's help, live the abundant life. But, we have to make decisions about that life. Seasonally, I go through my calendar, organizational memberships and some friendship associations. I decide if these projects/events are worth my time. Resurrect it by recommitting yourself to these projects. Bury it by resigning from that committee, disassociating yourself with certain people or taking that event off your calendar this year. Time is the one thing that we cannot afford to waste. Make critical decisions and stick to the decision you make. Decide today to start living the abundant life by answering the question should I resurrect it or bury it?

Thought of the Day:

Decisions are critical to reach certain destinations and vital to reach your destiny.

Reflection

"Now then, just as the LORD promised, he has kept me alive for forty-five years since the time he said this to Moses, while Israel moved about in the wilderness. So here I am today, eighty-five years old!"
Joshua 14:10 (NIV)

Right on Time

There are times in life when you run late. You got up on time but, the pants didn't fit right and you had to change so you ran late. Or maybe, you misplaced your keys and in the searching, you ran late. Have you ever thought that you were running late on the dreams of your life? You feel like you should be further along in your spiritual walk, career or the plans God intended for your life? You spent years in a relationship that didn't end in an "I do" or even a few more dates. Now you feel like you are late arriving or missed the one God intended for you. Or maybe, you put off going to school because you just wanted to work and do school later.

Now others, who are less talented but, qualified on paper, are further ahead of you in spite of the many more years you've been with the company. You feel like you're late. Or maybe, you just didn't want to accept the plan God had for you and ran from the assignment. Now, you're ready to complete the assignment with your whole heart. Let me assure you that you may feel like you're late but, you are right on time, for what God has designed for your life. God is infinite and orchestrating the affairs of your life in spite of you and time. Time means nothing to God. Preparing you for His divine purpose and you fulfilling His purpose, is His top priority. While you were spending time with the unnecessary relationship or trying to get yourself ready for school, He was preparing the position, person and path for you. As long as you are still alive God can use you. This is not an excuse for procrastination or disobedience but, a place to praise God for grace, mercy and longsuffering on His part. He didn't give up on His plan for you. He was waiting on you to yield yourself to His will, way and the word that He spoke over your life before you were born.

In the words of an old church song, "Yes, Lord from the bottom of my heart to the depths of my soul it's yes Lord, completely yes, my soul says yes."

Thought of the Day:

God is the best transportation system ever. He always gets you there and it will be right on time.

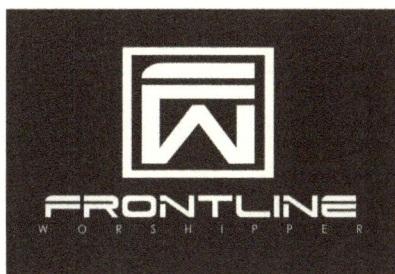

Reflection

_____

_____

_____

_____

_____

_____

_____

_____

_____

_____

_____

_____

_____

_____

_____

_____

_____

_____

_____

_____

"Let your speech be always with grace, seasoned with salt, that ye may know how ye ought to answer every man." Colossians 4:6 (KJV)

Seasoned Well, Slow Cooked and Served to Perfection

There is nothing like a pot of beans seasoned well with a smoked turkey bone in a crock pot cooked, slow and low all night. In the morning the house is filled with the aroma. Make some hot water corn bread, coleslaw and your meal is complete. There is nothing like a brisket that has been seasoned well and smoked for hours in a smoker with mesquite wood. The meat can be cut easily with a fork to complete a meal or can be added between two slices of bread for a wonderful sandwich. Before you stop reading and go to the kitchen, have you ever had a poorly cooked, dry, bland tasting meal? The meat was burned on the outside, raw on the inside and no seasoning to appeal to the taste buds.

Even though the vegetables had been in a pot on the stove, they were so crunchy they were raw and had no seasoning. You get my point. A well prepared meal takes time, attention, good ingredients and cooked at the proper temperature to satisfy. To be a well prepared person, it will take time, training and testing. There are people that you meet and immediately you know that they are not prepared. Others have their emotions supersede their ability which has left them burned on the outside, raw on the inside and unappealing to an employment or relationship pallet. You need to be seasoned with skills, experiences, tools and mentors so that you can do your best. You need to be slow cooked in an oven of trial and error, mistakes and victories in order to learn and do better next time. Microwaves may get you a meal in a hurry but, a gourmet meal must be prepared slow and with care on a stove by an experienced chef. There is a higher price to be well prepared but, when you are served or introduced to the world, it will be worth it.

Season your life knowledge and training, slow cook yourself in the stove of experience and mentorship, so that you will be served to perfection.

Thought of the Day:

Season your life with laughter, leisure and love.

Reflection

_____

_____

_____

_____

_____

_____

_____

_____

_____

_____

_____

_____

_____

_____

_____

_____

_____

_____

"While he was saying this to me, I bowed with my face toward the ground and was speechless." Daniel 10:15 (NIV)

"He says, Be still, and know that I am God..." Psalm 46:10 (NIV)

Speechless

There are several traditional songs that talk about when I get to heaven I am going to put on my robe, put on my shoes, run around God's heaven and tell this person my story. I don't know what I am going to do when I get to heaven but I will probably be speechless. In Daniel 10, Daniel had a visitation from an angel who was sent from God to deliver a message. When Daniel saw the angel, he bowed down and was speechless. Daniel was able to hear and submit to the word from the angel. There are times in God's presence where there is nothing that can be said. You can't utter a prayer, the name Jesus won't come out and you are rendered speechless. I believe that these are the times that God wants to transfer His spirit, power and presence deeper into your soul.

My prayer is to be able to hear God's voice clearly. I don't want to be consumed with my own thoughts and miss his voice to make the next move. When you don't know what to say in prayer, be reminded of the psalmist in Psalm 46:10, be still and know that I am God. Don't say anything just open your heart and spirit to what God wants to do in and through you. Bow down and remain speechless.

Thought of the Day:

Render your mouth speechless, to hear His voice clearly and move with precision.

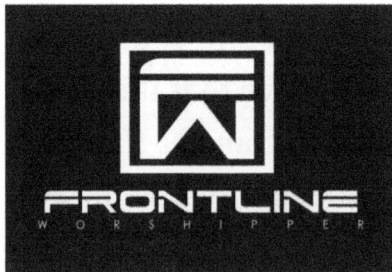

Reflection

"He that hath knowledge spareth his words: and a man of understanding is of an excellent spirit." Proverbs 17:27 (KJV)

"Then this Daniel was preferred above the presidents and princes, because an excellent spirit was in him…" Daniel 6:3 (KJV)

Spirit of Excellence or an Excellent Spirit?

The word "of" is a preposition defined as "from" something else. So the spirit of excellence would mean that the spirit is from excellence and not necessarily excellent. Excellent is defined as superior, extraordinary, worthy, first-rate or prime. In the bible, Daniel is described as one who was selected or preferred because he possessed an excellent, worthy or superior spirit. His spirit was not "of" excellence but, was excellent. Do you desire the spirit of excellence or a spirit that is excellent? For many years the phrase "spirit of excellence" was adopted as a customer service motto by corporate America as well as the ministry of administration.

As we have discovered, the spirit *of* excellence would mean that the spirit comes *from* excellence but, is not always excellent. People who perform in the spirit of excellence can perform well but, at times, the results are clouded with an arrogant, haughty or nasty spirit. We can't always enjoy the final project, performance or product. As we live our daily lives, let us desire and strive for an excellent spirit not just a "spirit of excellence." Just as Daniel was preferred and favored because of his excellent spirit, the favor of God will rest and rule with you when you possess an excellent spirit.

Thought of the Day:
Give God your excellence and don't compare your excellence with someone else's.

Reflection

_____

_____

_____

_____

_____

_____

_____

_____

_____

_____

_____

_____

_____

_____

_____

_____

_____

_____

_____

_____

_____

"But you asked GOD for help and he gave you the victory. GOD is always on the alert, constantly on the lookout for people who are totally committed to him."
2 Chronicles 16:7 (The Message)

Stop Watching and Ask for Help

There are some people that can use technology more easily than others. Some people can be shown how to operate the equipment and with little instruction perform the task. Others have to be shown repeatedly before they can perform the task on their own. When introducing a young group of students to logging onto the computers, some grasp the concept easier than others. When walking the room after the instruction, I noticed that the students that had difficulty with their assignment, stopped trying. Instead of asking for help, they stopped and started watching their neighbor already logged in use the software or website. Each student has his own computer and does not have to share, so the student is not waiting for their turn, just sitting there watching someone else. All of the students have the same computer, same software, same access and same teacher. Some will get more accomplished because they are willing to ask for help instead of giving up when it becomes hard and start watching others. This is true of some people who find certain things difficult. When a situation or task gets hard, they give up and start watching others do what they could be doing with a little help. What are you watching people do that you should be doing yourself? Do you need a little direction, guidance or encouragement? Raise your hand and ask the teacher. He never sleeps, never gets tired and loves to hear from His students. Stop watching, ask for help and start doing what God has called you to do.

Thought of the Day:

Those who ask for help and receive it are made wiser. Those who don't ask at all remain stagnant. Those who ask for help and don't receive it must be strong even to continue seeking.

Reflection

"And when he had looked round about on them with anger, being grieved for the hardness of their hearts, he saith unto the man, stretch forth thine hand. And he stretched it out: and his hand was restored whole as the other." Mark 3:5 (NIV)

"But lift thou up thy rod, and stretch out thine hand over the sea, and divide it." Exodus 14:16 (KJV)

Stretch Forth

Both Mark 3:5 and Exodus 14:16 give the account of two instances of two men with seemingly impossible situations. In Exodus, Moses is leading the children of Israel out of Egypt and they are now trapped at the Red Sea. In Mark, a man has a withered hand and can't use it to be productive and make a living for himself. Both men feel trapped by their situation but, in both cases were instructed to stretch out their hand to receive a miracle. Moses had a rod in his hand the Red Sea was parted and the children of Israel walked on dry land. The other man had nothing in his hand but, his withered hand was fully restored.

The power was in neither the rod or the man's hand but, in the simple act of obedience to stretching forth their hand. God's power was released through obedience. What do you have in your hand? It may not seem like much but, stretch it forth unto God.

Stretch forth your mind to believe that God can solve any problem or meet any need.

Stretch forth your actions to obey God's commandments

Stretch forth your resources to be used with wisdom for His Kingdom through your prosperity.

Stretch forth yourself to be a vessel of honor for God's glory and the edification of God's people.

Thought of the Day:

Stretch forth what's in your hand and watch God release what's in His.

Reflection

_____

_____

_____

_____

_____

_____

_____

_____

_____

_____

_____

_____

_____

_____

_____

_____

_____

_____

_____

Therefore, although in Christ I could be bold and order you to do what you ought to do, yet I appeal to you on the basis of love. I then, as Paul—an old man and now also a prisoner of Christ Jesus—I appeal to you for my son Onesimus,[a] who became my son while I was in chains. Formerly he was useless to you, but now he has become useful both to you and to me." Philemon 1:8-11 (NIV)

User, Useless or Useful

As the seasons change, I take inventory with regards to my purpose, people in my life and my productivity. I inventory ministry materials, music and messages to see what may be necessary for upcoming events. I also list my unfinished work on started projects. I also inventory relationships and determine their value, importance and pray for direction for their continuation and/or elimination in the future. Paul in Philemon was aging and he was preparing himself, his ministry and his followers for his death. He was taking inventory of the people that were a part of his ministry.

In Philemon 1, Paul is giving a recommendation for Onesimus. It appears that early on, Onesimus was not ready for ministry and was referred to as useless. But, after mentoring, encouragement and growth, was now ready to be useful for ministry. So Paul said receive Onesimus now because he can be very useful to you and me in ministry. Are you useful or useless to your friends and/or people around you? When people see you coming do they say, "help is here" or "hindrance is here?" I recently received a text from a friend who said that he was taking inventory of his friends and weeding out people who were just users. So I ask you, are you useful, useless or just a user?

Think about it...

Thought of the Day:

To be useful is to be used for a purpose that not only helps others but, you feel fulfilled and proud of the work that you have done.

Reflection

_____
_____
_____
_____
_____
_____
_____
_____
_____
_____
_____
_____
_____
_____
_____
_____
_____
_____
_____
_____

"He has taken me to the banquet hall, and his banner over me is love." Song of Solomon 2:4 (NIV)

What Does Your Banner Say?

When coming out of my house one day, I noticed that there was a flag or banner waving outside a house down the street. The banner read, "stay cool." This banner served as a humorous reminder since we experienced extremely hot temperatures this summer. Other houses wave the American flag proudly and still others' homes have a banner that represents their favorite sports team. Solomon in the Song of Solomon states that God's banner over him is love. We know that God loves us all. But, God's goes further in that His very nature is love. Love is not just what God does, it is what God is. What do you want the banner at your house to say? Dependable people live here. Kind people live here. Mean people live here. Liars live here. Believers live here. A house in the bible represents your life.

Would others agree with the banner over your house or life? The house with the American flag has a resident that may be a veteran or simply loves America. The house with the sports team logo and/or mascot wants people to know that they support a specific team. What does the banner over your life really say?

Challenge: Design a banner for your life.

Materials needed:

Blank paper

Crayons, colored pencils or markers

What does your banner look like?

Thought of the Day:

Live your life so that when you wave your banner people will want to agree with what your banner says.

Reflection

_____

_____

_____

_____

_____

_____

_____

_____

_____

_____

_____

_____

_____

_____

_____

_____

_____

_____

_____

"Put on the whole armour of God, that ye may be able to stand against the wiles of the devil."
Ephesians 6:11 (KJV)

What Should You Be Wearing?

We live in a very visual society and appearance is a key asset to your success. The top two on the list of commercial success in business is 1) academic or experiential qualifications and 2) appearance and presentation. Depending upon the industry, this top two list can be inter-changeable in priority. There is a television show called, "What not to wear" hosted by two fashion stylists who are attempting to change the appearance and style of a person nominated by family, friends and co-workers. Someone has videotaped the person wearing their current clothing, their home closet and a message expressing how they hate the clothes their friend wears. The person's current wardrobe is either out of style, too large, too small or just wrong.

The person chosen for the "makeover" is usually successful, educated and equipped academically but, has no clue about what to wear. What should you be wearing that will represent you and your savior in the best light?

"...be clothed with humility...." I Peter 5:5 (KJV)

"...be clothed with salvation...."
2 Chronicles 6:41 (KJV)

"Awake, awake, put on strength..."
Isaiah 51:9 (KJV)

"I put on righteousness, and it clothed me..."
Job 29:14 (KJV)

"...let us put on the armour of light."
Romans 13:12 (KJV)

"For as many of you as have been baptized into Christ have put on Christ." Galatians 3:27 (KJV)

"And that ye put on the new man..."
Ephesians 4:24 (KJV)

Put on therefore, as the elect of God, holy and beloved, bowels of mercies, kindness, humbleness of mind, meekness, longsuffering;
Colossians 3:12 (KJV)

"And above all these things put on charity, which is the bond of perfectness."
Colossians 3:14 (KJV)

Thought of the Day:

Clothes don't make the man but, the clothes tell us something about the man.

Reflection

www.ingramcontent.com/pod-product-compliance
Lightning Source LLC
Chambersburg PA
CBHW020851090426
42736CB00008B/334